Amelia Flies

by **Anne Phillips**

·

illustrated by
Laurie Harden

MODERN CURRICULUM PRESS

Pearson Learning Group

Amelia Earhart was born in 1897 in a house full of books. As a girl, Amelia loved to read. She would even recite poems while she swept the floor. But Amelia loved to do other things too.

When Amelia was young, most people thought girls should wear dresses and play with dolls. Amelia's parents didn't think so. So she and her sister wore loose pants called bloomers. In her bloomers, Amelia climbed and raced and squatted down to look at worms and toads. She played ball. She fished. She rode horses.

Once Amelia built a roller coaster. She was the test pilot for the first ride. She threw herself down the track and crashed. But that didn't make her more cautious. Being cautious just wasn't Amelia's style. She fixed the roller coaster until it worked.

"It's just like flying!" she cried.

Even at school Amelia was in a hurry. The principal thought that if Amelia showed all the steps in her math work she could win a math prize. Amelia thought writing down the steps took too long. She told the principal to let some other student have the prize.

5

Amelia was ten when she saw her first airplane. Later she saw stunt pilots make dangerous spins and dives. She loved it! Even when she went away to college, she could not stop thinking about flying.

Amelia began working and saved enough money to take flying lessons. In 1922, she got her pilot's license. There were only a few women pilots in the world at the time.

What did it take to be a pilot? You had to know how to fly, of course. You had to be able to fly in snow, rain, and fog. But you had to know how to work on the engine of your plane too.

Amelia continued to learn more about flying. She learned how to make her plane spin and dive. She learned how to land with the engine off. That way, if her engine stopped working, she would be able to land safely.

8

In 1928, Amelia became the first woman to fly across the Atlantic Ocean. But she did not pilot the plane. Two men flew the plane. Amelia just rode along with them.

It was a dangerous flight. The fog made it hard to see where they were going. The radio went dead. And it got worse! Before they reached land, the plane began to run out of fuel.

9

Finally the plane landed in the sea near the coast of Wales. They had made it! When they reached the shore, they heard chanting.

People had gathered on the shore to welcome them. Crowds were chanting, "Amelia! Amelia!"

After this flight, Amelia was famous. But she didn't feel very brave. All she had done was ride across the ocean. And Amelia still was not a cautious person. She wanted to pilot her own plane across the Atlantic.

So she trained and trained. In 1932 she took off on her own to cross the ocean.

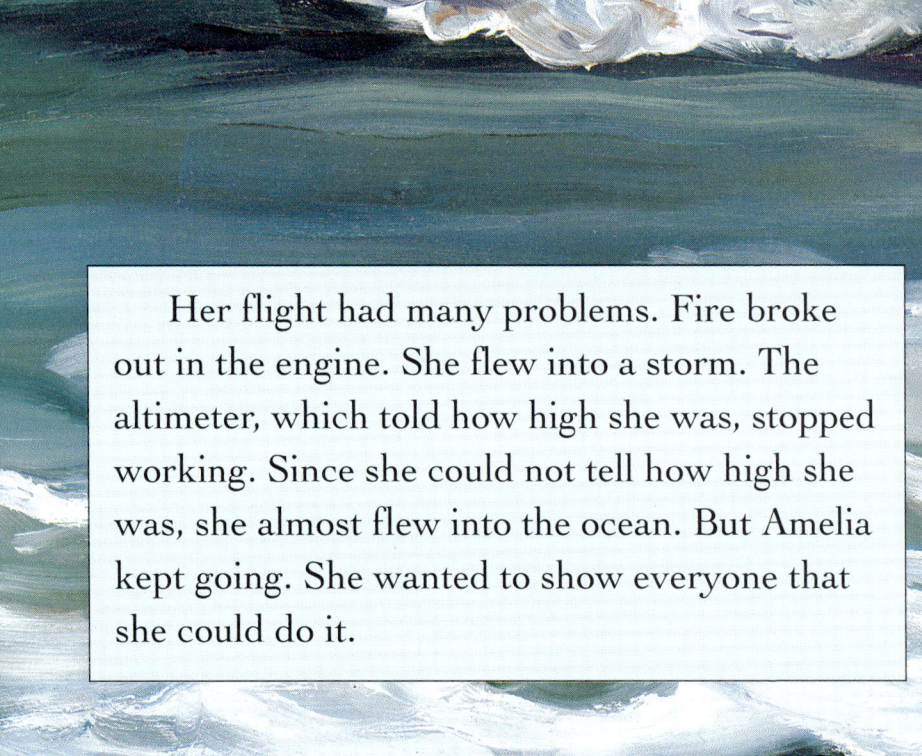

Her flight had many problems. Fire broke out in the engine. She flew into a storm. The altimeter, which told how high she was, stopped working. Since she could not tell how high she was, she almost flew into the ocean. But Amelia kept going. She wanted to show everyone that she could do it.

At last Amelia saw land. She landed her plane in Ireland. She was now the first woman to fly alone across the Atlantic!

"It may not be all smooth sailing," she said. "But the fun of it is worth the price."

Amelia would continue to make more flights and set new records. She was the first woman to fly from Hawaii to the mainland. And she was the first to fly alone across the United States—in both directions!

There was still one flight Amelia wanted to make. She wanted to fly around the world.

After careful planning, Amelia and her navigator took off from California. They flew from South America to Africa and then to Australia. But the most dangerous part of the trip lay ahead.

The plane headed for Howland Island in the Pacific Ocean. But it never got there. Somewhere over the Pacific, the plane just vanished. Ships and planes searched for Amelia and her navigator. But they were never found. Most people think the plane crashed in the ocean and sank.

15

Before she left on her last flight, Amelia wrote a letter. In it she told why she was making the dangerous trip.

"I want to do it because I want to do it," Amelia wrote. "Women must try to do things as men have tried. When they fail, their failure must be but a challenge to others."

In her life, Amelia Earhart was the first woman to do many things that men had done. She was one of the women who led the way for others.